MONEY
MAKING CLICKS

Step-by-Step Instructions to
Take Your Business Online
to Profit from Internet Advertising

SVEN HOLMBOM

Interior Graphics by Eric Olmos.

ISBN: 978-1-4834-8015-2 (sc)
ISBN: 978-1-4834-8014-5 (e)

Library of Congress Control Number: 2018901142

Lulu Publishing Services rev. date: 04/19/2018

Acknowledgment

Thank you for you support and encouragement:
Isa, Amelia, Otto, Erik, Silvia and Peter W

Table of Contents

First Things First

Today, almost any implementation of an idea starts with a quick search on the Internet. It is the obvious place to be and to be seen. Get started now. This book is a crash course in basic Internet principles and the fundamentals of Internet marketing, meant to be basic and easy to understand. If you follow these simple tips, you can move your business or service to Internet-based marketing, a guaranteed game changer.

The algorithm that Google uses for its search network is a well-guarded secret. However, Google's fundamental principles are very straightforward. I will provide you with some industry standards and common practices that will help you understand enough to start developing your own on-line strategies in the future.

Advertising has changed enormously in the past few years, diverting its focus from traditional print, TV, and radio to the new media: the Internet. The beauty of Internet marketing is that you only market to the people who are sincerely interested in your product or service and actively looking for it. With a well-run campaign, you only pay when someone clicks on your ad and arrives at your website. You never pay for clicks you don't get.

There are many reasons a typical brick-and-mortar, mom-and-pop shop can be very successful in applying digital marketing. They know the business inside out and the inventory is already there. Once they develop a strong presence on the Internet, all they need to do is to start accepting new payment methods and offer new ways to deliver products or services.

When I started out a few years ago, there was very little information on Internet marketing and had to figure it out myself. Today, on the other hand, you are bombarded with too much information and content that might be overwhelming. This basic book is the perfect tool to guide you in the right direction so you can finally get it done and get your business on line with very simple instructions.

So, Let's Get Started with Some Basics

As you probably already know, when you go on the Web to look for something, you use a Web browser such as Chrome, Firefox or Safari, to name a few.

You visit websites that are ultimately located on special computers called servers or hosts. In order to host your website, you must rent a space on one of these Web servers. Think of it as a cloud service, where you can upload, download, and keep stuff on the Internet. There are many options for hosting your site, from free to expensive and including very specialized super servers. As with everything else, you usually get what you pay for.

> *TIP:*
> *Choose your hosting service with care and protect yourself with more than basic security and backups. Once your website is successful in bringing in clients and business, getting hacked or going off-line can be a traumatic and expensive experience.*

Domain Names and URLs

To find a specific server and a specific page, domain names are used, just as you would use an address in a town or city. A domain name is the name of your business on the Internet, as in these examples:

cnn.com
coca-cola.com

A Uniform Resource Locator, abbreviated as URL, is a web address. It is a specific character string that is used to get visitors to any specific page within your domain name. Take a look at these two examples of URLs:

cnn.com/technology
coca-cola.com/our-company

The Anatomy of a URL

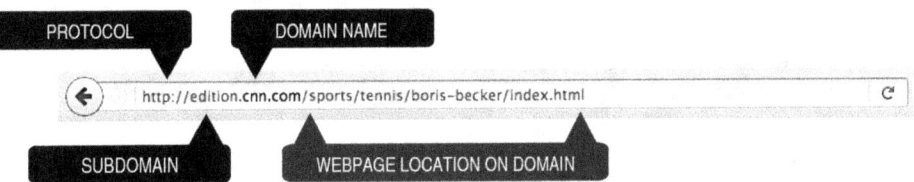

So how do Web pages know who you are and how to find you? The secret is in the IP address (that stands for "Internet Protocol"). This is a string of numbers assigned to every device hooked up to the Internet, Web servers among them. There are two major types of IPs: dynamic and static. A static IP never changes. However, your personal devices, including mobiles, laptops, tablets, and computers, typically have dynamic IP addresses that change every time you hook up to the Internet. The initial numbers in the address indicate the country where you are at the moment and reveal almost your exact location. Thanks to this information, it is possible to market to users in specific geographical locations. We will talk more about this later.

Understanding the nature of a URL is vital to all future examples in this book.

Once you find a domain name that you like, register it immediately. Do not wait. If you do, it might be taken because automatic services register domains recently searched but not yet registered. These services then register the names in the hope of selling them later at a higher price. Once you have chosen a name, it is a good idea to also register similar variations and comparable domain names. Also register your domain ending with .com, .net, and .us or other countries.

Domain names are not expensive, just a few dollars, so go for it and make it hard for your competition to steal your idea and set up a similar business model. Just register the domain on the server that you will be using to host your webpage. Normally, you can park all the domains you want on your server at no extra cost.

You Should Be the Owner of Your Domain Name

This might sound obvious but if you let the person or company building your website register your domain name, you may not be able to get it back if you stop using their services. Make sure the domain is yours. Also make sure you or your company has all the main passwords to the hosting service. This might also sound basic, but it is just as important as giving the key to the main door of your home or business to someone you trust. Your server password should be treated as securely as the PIN code of your credit card or cell phone. Do not give the password to anyone. Instead, create additional users on the server and give them access, at your discretion, with their own passwords.

> *TIP:*
> *A well-run website is an asset to your company and can be a very good business. The investments you make online deserve the same attention as other assets of your company, such as a storefront, new equipment, and so on.*

Building a Website

There are many free website builders that allow you to set up your website yourself. They might fulfill your purpose, and assembling different elements and thinking about how you want your site to look and feel can be a good exercise. These do-it-yourself builders like WIX, Web.com, Sitebuilder.com and Weebly are usually very user-friendly. However, a word of caution: as the old saying goes, "There is no free lunch." You will find that some have ads on the websites, which is not a good idea. Even your competitors could advertise on your site, therefore, I don't recommend having ads you can't control on your website at all.

In the early days, standalone HTML (the language that makes a web browser understand a web page) pages were the standard. Now most use an application installed on the hosting server called a Content Management System (CMS). Just as it sounds, a CMS manages digital content and allows you to build a complete website without the need for coding at all. The program will do the coding for you.

Usually a CMS has two major components. The first is the back end, where you log in and manage your content as documents, movies, pictures, phone numbers, and other elements that can be added or removed from the website. This can normally be done without the help of a webmaster.

Then there is the front end, which delivers the updated information and content to the site visitor. Often the design you see on the page is from a template that uses a code called CSS. Editing a few lines in the CSS file can change the graphic design (layout, colors, and fonts) of one page or all the pages on your website.

There are thousands of templates for free or reasonably priced with fantastic designs. Usually you can find a specific template already made for your type of business, which can be a good starting point.

URLs are important when it comes to performing well with Google, so keeping them unchanged for the long term is vital to the success of the page. It can be difficult to maintain exactly the same URLs when changing a platform or rebuilding a website. You don't want to end up having to build your reputation all over again with Google when you rebuild elsewhere.

In 2015, due to the mobile explosion with smartphones, Google released a significant new algorithm designed to penalize pages that are not mobile friendly. Keep this in mind, and make sure your page is mobile friendly so as not to lose page rank (which is later explained). This is done by having a template with a responsive design, which means that the page will adapt dynamically according to the screen size of the device accessing your page. Remember this when choosing a template!

In 2018 Google will start indexing the mobile content of a website before the "desktop content" and will primarily use the mobile version of a site's content to rank its pages. This mobile-first index is a major shift in how the search result are presented. If your website is mobile friendly with responsive design you are ready for the mobile-first index.

A CMS also enables the use of extensions and plugins. These are small programs you can install to perform specific tasks, such as a shopping cart, booking reservations, photo albums, and polls. Other advantages, that we will explain in more detail further down, are SEO-friendly URLs, integrated and online help, and installation and upgrade wizards. The most popular CMS is WordPress. There are also Joomla, Drupal, and hundreds more. Many of the most popular ones are "open source", so they are free of charge. (See more about open source in the last chapter).

TIP:
This is a test you can run to see if your page is mobile friendly: google.com/test/mobile-friendly.

SEO-friendly URLs are those you can easily read and understand (and Google can understand). This is a good one: www.yahoo.com/**news**/. This is a bad one: www.yahoo.com/**item/235687**. The format makes a big difference when you start advertising because your URL is part of the ad.

Landing page, The Secret To Success!

Most probably, your visitors will get to your website through an ad of some sort. They will come to a specific page. That page, called a **landing page**, should be prepared with a lot of care and must have a SEO-friendly URL. Poorly designed websites give the impression that you don't care about your business or your customers. Your website needs to be more appealing than your competitors'. In a short glimpse, your visitor will decide whether to stay on the page or to move on and maybe find a better page. More than 70% of all web visitors leave the first page and take no further action – this is called a **Bounce**.

The Landing Page should be very relevant to the specific **Search Query**, which are the words that are typed into a search engine which, in turn, triggered the ad. Try to think exactly what the visitor is looking for and tailor the content and experience as close to that as possible. It will also help you with the ranking of your page (Google Page Rank) and you will get more clicks and visitors to your page (Click Through Rate), the perfect combination for a successful website.

> *TIP:*
> *Importance of a good landing page: A good Landing Page has original and relevant content, fast loading time with a minimum of pop-ups. It is easy to navigate.*

SEO Basics

Search Engine Optimization (SEO) is the process of getting the page to perform better on search engines without paying for it—often referred to as **"natural" or "organic" ranking** results. SEO will significantly increase the number of visitors to your page. This is a complicated *science* but here are some basic guidelines.

For Google to understand that your page is relevant to a search, it must have a certain structure.

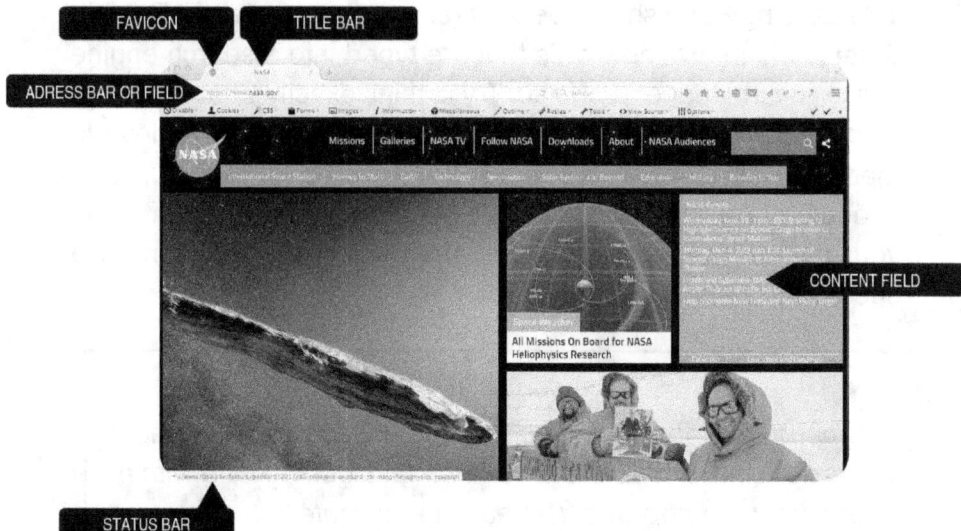

The Anatomy Of a Web Browser.

1. **Title Bar** – The text in the upper left corner is called the title bar. This should describe the content of the website or webpage. The text in the title bar is also the text that appears in Google search results in the headline
2. **Address Bar or Field** – Where the URL, or web address, appears. It also serves as a search box in most browsers.
3. **Content Field** – Where the content of the page is displayed, including texts, pictures, graphics and others.
4. **Status Bar** – A horizontal bar, located at the bottom of the page showing information about a page before it is loaded. You can even see where the link loading is actually taking you.
5. **Favicon** – A small iconic image representing your brand or website. I think the term is a shortening of "favorite

icon." It will appear in tabs and bookmarks. You must install it yourself in the CMS.

If text and other content coincide in these five areas, your page is doing very well for SEO. In other words, keywords and the description of the page accurately represent the text and information on the page. That is good for Google ranking.

Click-through rate (CTR)

Click-through rate (CTR) is determined by the percentage of people who actually click on a specific link, versus the total number of people who are exposed to that page or ad (impressions) This is the most common way to measure on line success.

CTR = Impressions / Clicks

Metadata and Meta Descriptions

The information about your website used by search engines such as Google, Yahoo, Ask to determine the relevance of your page is called **Metadata** and should be embedded in the code of your web page. This means that the embedded text will not appear in your normal view of the page with your browser.

An advantage of using a CMS application is that it is very easy to add Meta Descriptions, keywords and analytics code, in preset areas.

Below you can find an example of how the embedded HTML text looks with the coding made by the CMS. Remember, a web browser only displays what the code instructs it to display.

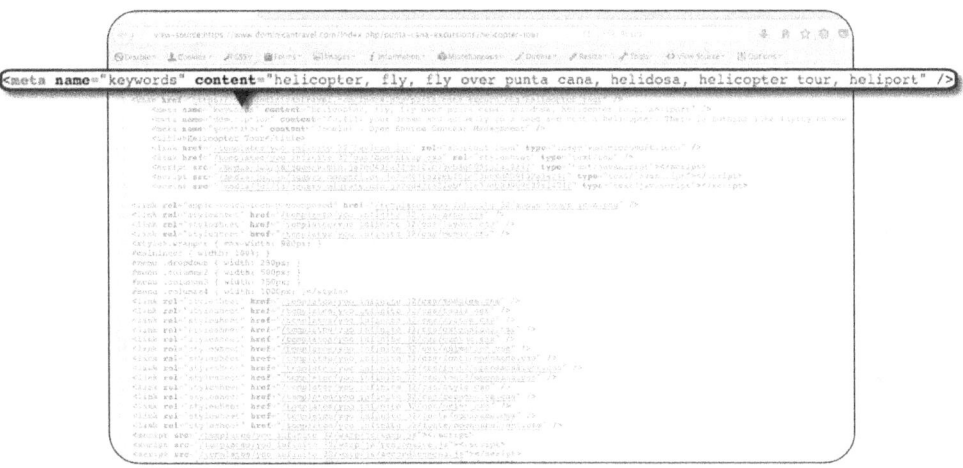

You should have about 10 to 15 keywords (those you want to be found by) in the embedded text in the HTML code. They should be in lower caps and separated by a comma and no plurals. Google understands plurals and misspelled words.

The embedded text should also contain the **Meta Description**, a brief description summarizing a webpage's content, in a maximum 160 characters. Search engines use these in search results to let you know what a page is about before clicking on it.

EXAMPLE: See below how Google's Meta Description describes the site's purpose

Google
https://www.google.com/ ▾
Search the world's information, including webpages, images, videos and more. Google has many special features to help you find exactly what you're looking for.

Backlinks

Links to your webpage from other pages are called Backlinks and are by some considered very good, especially if they are from authoritative and relevant sites. This can help you get traffic referred to your site and help you with Google's organic ranking.

> *TIP:*
> *Manipulating the number of links pointing to the page is an example of Black Hat SEO. These techniques involve artificially increasing the ranking of a webpage linking fake links to the page. Google's Guidelines are against this and it is penalized by Google algorithms. They have specialized programs called Google Penguin and Google Panda to deter this practice. It is also considered bad practice to use misspelled words and other tricks to try to get traffic to your page, so I strongly recommend not to do that.*

Let Google Know That You Have a Website

To inform Google that you have a new, great site with relevant content, you should register with Google Webmasters and submit the content of your site organized into what is called a **sitemap**, containing all the structure and content of the site. By doing so, Google understands the content of all your pages right away, instead of waiting for Google to crawl your page which can take much longer.

Having a good sitemap will also help the navigation experience of your visitors to find things on your site.

The sitemap should be in XML protocol, to allow changes to the content of your page to be automatically updated with Google. Most CMS will automatically make an XML sitemap of your site to be submitted to Google Webmaster. It is as easy, as just opening an account and entering the link to the sitemap on your page. Just to be clear, you need two sitemaps, one that is easy to find on your page for your visitors, and one XML for Google webmaster.

If you have a very large site with many pages, **breadcrumbs** (or breadcrumb trail) can greatly enhance the way users find their way around sections and pages. The term comes from the Hansel and Gretel fairy tale in which the two title children drop breadcrumbs to form a trail back to their home. Basically, it is a visual trail for the user to follow back to the starting point or previous pages to understand where on the site they are. Most CMS will provide this automatically if activated.

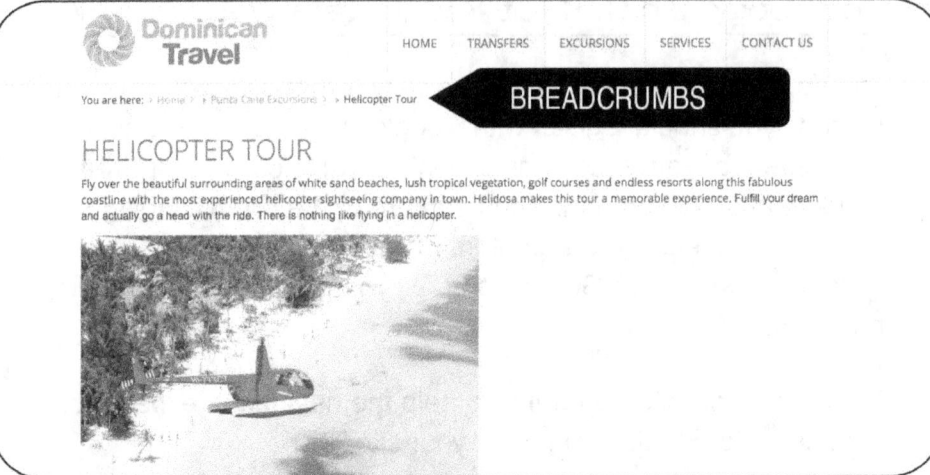

Few Pay Attention to The Importance of The Fold:

What you see on your screen is called **Above the Fold**, the rest of the Web page that you must scroll down to see, is called **Below the Fold**. Make sure that your most important message is always on Top of The Fold, to avoid a high bounce rate when visitors don't find right away what they are looking for. Later on, I will explain how you can place all your ads **Above the Fold** (also called Above the Scroll) to make sure they are seen right away.

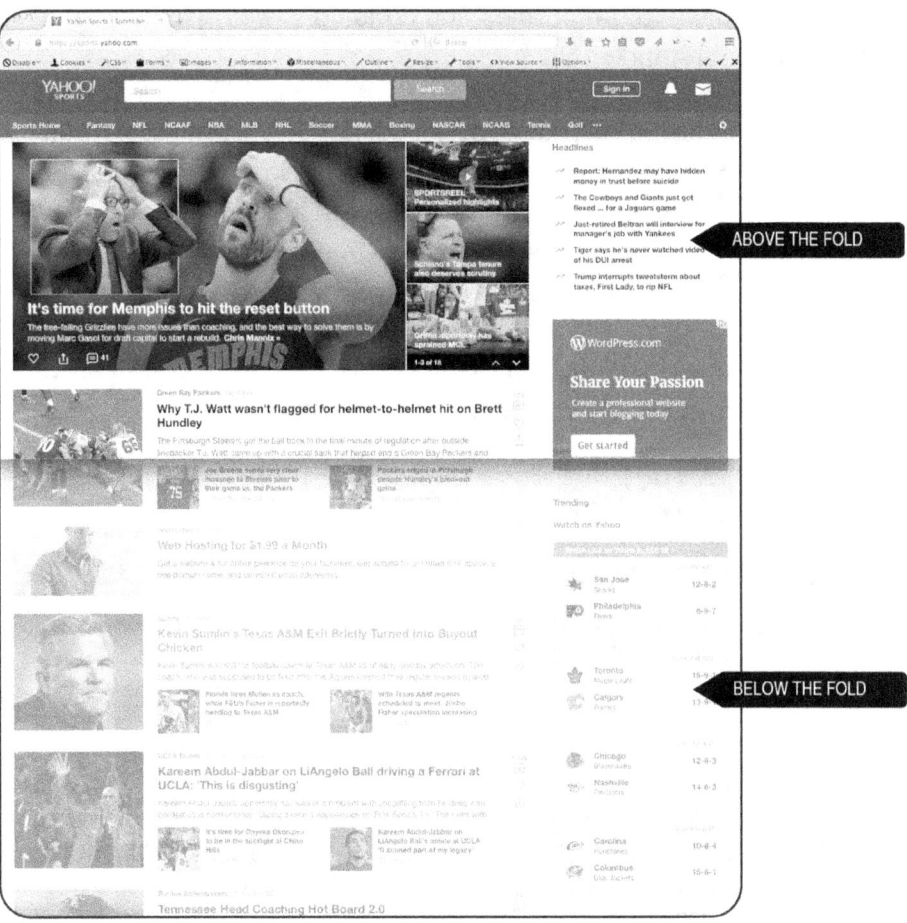

Trust

Trust is vital!! First, Google must trust your page in order to send traffic to your site, but also the visitor to your page must trust you to buy from you. Positive customer ratings and testimonials, as well as logos and endorsements from reputable organizations you might belong to, are ways to generate trust. Also try to tell your story, have return policies and conditions well displayed and easy to understand.

Another way to build trust is by installing SSL Certificates that provide secure, encrypted communication between a website and an Internet browser. The easiest is to buy the digital certificate from reputable companies dedicated to the service, which you can then then install on your server or hosting service.

The protocol will change from Http:// to Https:// ending with an S and you will see a lock in the browser address bar.

Quick Access to Google Products

Google requires that you have an account registered with them to use their products and services. This account will allow access to Google services such as AdWords, Analytics, Google+, Gmail, Google Drive, Google Calendar and many other great products. The username you choose does not have to be a Gmail account and you can use any email to register, but if you have a Gmail account you are already registered with Google and you can use that account.

How to create a **Google account.**

1. Go to www.google.com.
2. In the upper right corner, click "Sign in"
3. Choose "Create an account". (If this option does not appear Click on "More Options" and then choose "Create an account").
4. Fill out the form to create your profile
5. After reviewing the Terms of Service and Conditions, agree by clicking on the box. At this point, there is a simple verification process with Google.
6. The account will be created, and you will see the Google welcome page. Click on the "Continue" button.

Know Your Metrics

Just as you have to know the numbers in your business you have to know the numbers of your web page; these statistics are called **Metrics.** The best available tool to measure everything on your page is Google Analytics. According to Google, the system "helps you analyze visitor traffic and paint a complete picture of your audience and their needs, wherever they are along the path to purchase". The more you know about the activities on the page, such as number of visitors, demographics, behavior, and so on, the better.

Analytics is also necessary to run a successful ad campaign on Google AdWords, because the most advanced campaigns require that both accounts are linked together. The best part of this tool is that it is 100% free.

Just open a Google Analytics account and follow the instructions. It is relatively easy to setup the account, but if it becomes initially overwhelming to set up, I really recommend getting professional help, even if there is a cost. This tool is absolutely necessary and will be your best ally to **measure your online activity.**

How Does Google Analytics Work?

It is an application connected to your website through a piece of tracking code or "Tag", which is a short script (called a snippet) embedded in the code of a web page. This collects user data and places cookies (small text files) in web browsers generating detailed statistics about activity on a website.

In Analytics you find the Tags by logging into your account and clicking the Admin tab. Then, under **Property**, go to **".js Tracking Info"**, to get the Tracking Code. Just copy and paste the whole code (that appears in a box) into the HTML on your web page.

In the graph below, you can see an example of a Tracking Code. A Tracking ID is a number-letter combination code which is part of the Tracking Code and can be found at the bottom of the box (see picture). Most CMS let you place Tracking Codes automatically by pasting or inserting the Tracking ID into a preset field.

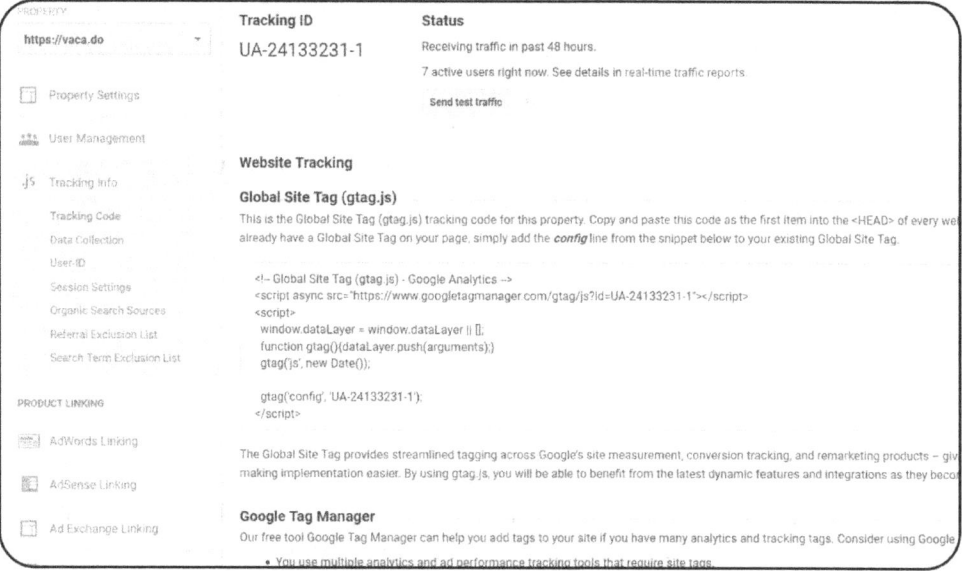

Google Tag Manager is a good place to manage your tags and have fewer tags on your page. The disadvantage of having too many tags is that they may slow down your website. Therefore, if you have several tags on your site, the Tag Manager gives you the option to put them in a container, where you can have several tags built into one.

When a tag is working properly, it is called "firing". You can test if the tag is firing, through your Google Analytics account. If you use Google Chrome browser, you can install an extension, the Google Tag Assistant, which will let you know if the tags are firing and placed at the correct location on the page.

Google has a strict policy about what information you can collect from a user and a computer. Personal data such as names, phone numbers and social security numbers are not allowed to be collected. Nonetheless, be aware that hackers and other ill-intentioned individuals can very possibly retrieve this information from your computer

> NOTE: EU (European Union) law requires all sites using cookies to seek visitors' consent to store and retrieve data about their browsing habits to guarantee their online privacy.

Opting Out of Tracking

You can opt out of tracking completely. This is a good idea if you do not want your own visits to be counted on your website, messing up the Analytics metrics. There are several ways to do this (Through IP addresses, making special cookies and other ways) I find that the easiest way is to use **Google Analytics Opt-out Browser Add-on,** which you download and install in your browser. It will tell Google Analytics JavaScript not to send data to Google Analytics. All your associates and employees should do the same, so that your visits to the page don't count.

This is the link where you find the Opt-Out Browser Add-On: https://tools.google.com/dlpage/gaoptout

Why Google Ads?

There are several ways to advertise on the Internet. Google is the world leader but there are also Bing and Yahoo to name a few. Since Google is the biggest and most widely used, this book focuses on Google AdWords. If you are still interested in advertising on Bing and Microsoft Network that manages the advertising on Yahoo, you can first set up an account with Google then import all the campaigns with all the settings and keywords to your Bing account. Cost for Ad bids on Bing tend to be lower than Google and less competition for keywords, so it makes it interesting to explore.

Both Google and Bing have editors that are applications which can be downloaded for free to manage your account offline. Then upload the changes to AdWords when you are back online. These editors are very useful when managing large campaigns that require a lot of changes and attention to many details.

What's a Search Network? What's a Display Network?

Google Ads are placed in two different networks: the Search Network and Display Network. Users are targeted by Search Ads as they conduct a routine search via the Search Network such as Yahoo, Ask, Bing and of course the main one, Google.

Ads placed on the Search Network are only text-based and have proven to be very effective, since they are shown to active searchers who are on a mission to find something on the web. With luck, they will click on your ad, related to their search.

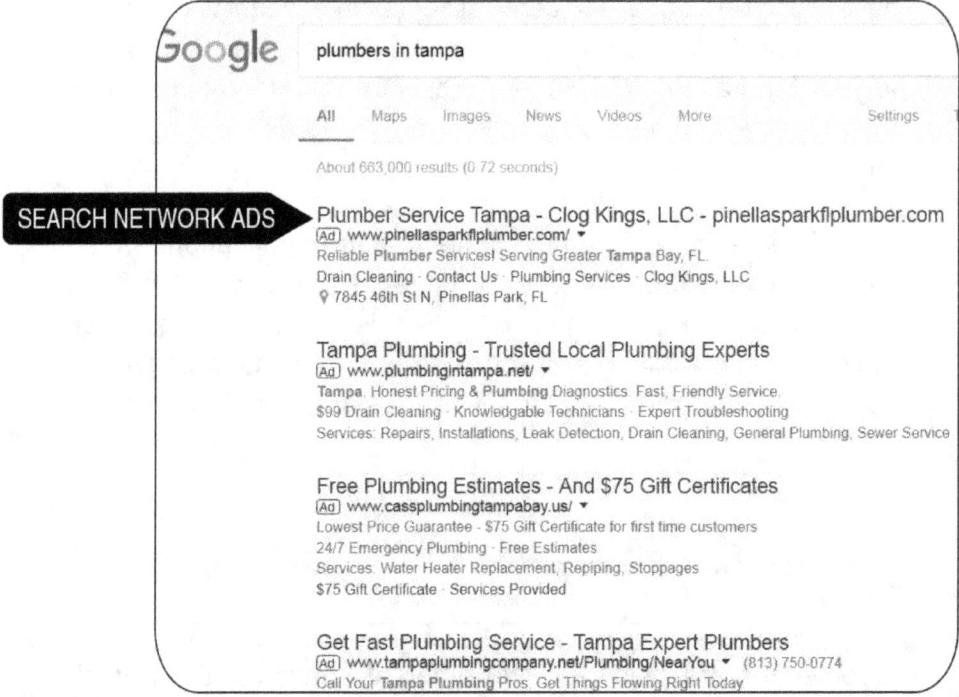

How to Reach the Top of the Search Network

Yes, there is actually a way around all the SEO and other optimization techniques" You can **pay your way** to the top of the search results.

As mentioned before, there are two types of ads. The most basic is a search ad. Here's how it works: When someone is searching and types in a question (called a search query or search term), the query is matched to a set of keywords that triggers an ad.

Ads are shown on the page in a specific order called the "ad position", which is determined by a quality score. The quality score is a combination of your **bid** (how much you are willing to pay for the ad to show) and **the ad's relevance** to the search, called **Ad Rank**. Ad Rank is directly affected by the quality of your website page, especially **the landing page**. That's the page where the visitor arrives on your site after clicking on an ad or search result listing.

Why Extensions Are Important

Extensions are extra bits of text information that you can include in your ads, such as phone numbers or a business location. There are also **callout extensions**. An example would be a special offer or some other attention grabber. Then there are **sitelink extensions**, which display specific information on your website. Extensions increase the CTR and improve ad visibility for a better return on investment (ROI). The expected CTR is how Google measures the success of your ad. It is determined by the amount of times your ad is shown (impressions) divided by the amount of clicks it receives. The actual Cost-Per-Click (CPC) will go down, as the Ad Rank goes up. There is no extra cost to add extensions, so the better the ads, the cheaper they will be.

Pay-per-click (PPC), also known as **cost per click (CPC)**, will display an advertisement when a keyword query matches an advertiser's keyword list.

> *TIP:*
> *A CTR over 2% is considered good as an industry standard, but you should aim much higher with a minimum of 7% - 8% by continually improving your ads and landing pages. It is actually possible to get a CTR of 20% - 30%. On the Display Network, CTR is significantly lower than the Search Network*

What is a Display Network?

A Display Network is any ad that you see on the Web across the huge network of sites available. The ads are displayed on millions of sites across the Web, many of which are trying to make money from the traffic on their site. More than 2 million websites have ads on them, covering 90% of all Internet users. You can decide where you want your ads to show, by topic or by a targeted audience (people that are already interested in your product or service). This beauty is called Re-Marketing and you can actually target potential customers that have already visited your webpage. This can be very effective as they are already familiar with your brand and interested in your product. It can be done by showing text, video, images or rich media that encourage the audience to interact with the ads, which sometimes tell a story. This advertising is done by sorting your clients (Web visitors) on lists that they sign up for automatically through cookies or Tags. You build the lists in shared libraries in your AdWords account.

In AdWords, Tags are found in Shared Libraries under the "audiences" section.

You decide yourself how long the visitor stays on the list and gets exposed to your ads. You do not want to bombard visitors with too many ads for too long. This can have a negative impact on your brand. The maximum time Google allows for a Remarketing list is 540 days, so you can get huge amounts of visitors and a very large audience to target.

As more people and companies are competing for the same space on the display network, the prices go up to place an ad. As with golf, once you start you are going to wish you had started earlier.

You can also block your ads from showing on websites in categories where you do not want them to appear, such as sites focused on gambling, tragedy or conflict. We will explain how to do in this detail in a later section.

> *TIP:*
> *In the Tools section of your AdWords account, you will find a Keyword Planner that can help you research keywords statistics and traffic forecasts. There is also a Display Planner that can estimate the possible reach and cost of your Display Network campaigns.*

What is a Remarketing Ad? What is an Advertising Banner?

Remarketing ads are shown to people that are interested in your product, based on their previous behavior on the web. Advertising Banners, **or banner ads,** are shown indiscriminately to everyone on the Web. Usually with banner ads, you pay for impressions and not for clicks.

When making one ad for the Display Network, you will actually need to make 20 adaptations of the same ad in different sizes, if you want it to be displayed in all available formats and on different devices and screen sizes.

Supported ad specs *(From Google)*.

File types Formats GIF, JPG, PNG, SWF, ZIP
Max. size 150KB - **NOTE Important!!**
Ad sizes Square and rectangle
200 × 200 Small square
240 × 400 Vertical rectangle
250 × 250 Square
250 × 360 Triple widescreen
300 × 250 Inline rectangle
336 × 280 Large rectangle
580 × 400 Netboard Skyscraper
120 × 600 Skyscraper
160 × 600 Wide skyscraper
300 × 600 Half-page ad
300 × 1050 Portrait Leaderboard
468 × 60 Banner
728 × 90 Leaderboard
930 × 180 Top banner
970 × 90 Large leaderboard
970 × 250 Billboard
980 × 120 Panorama Mobile
300 × 50 Mobile banner
320 × 50 Mobile banner
320 × 100 Large mobile banner

Ads that have movement in them usually get a higher CTR. **Google Web Designer** is a free tool that can be used to make ads with movement that run on mobile and all other platforms.

Setting up an AdWords Account

Go to https://adwords.google.com and click on the "Start now" button.

Follow the simple steps on your screen. You need to provide your email address and website URL again. AdWords will also send a verification code to your mobile phone (or voice call) to verify your new account. Then just walk through the setup process. Here you have to make some small decisions such as daily budget and location (where to advertise) and select a **search or display campaign**. (I recommend starting with a Search Network Only campaign.) You will also be asked to choose keywords (Google will likely suggest keywords to start) and your bid (Google can show this automatically). Next, choose the text for your first ad.

Finally, set up your payment method. Google will bill you when you reach your payment threshold, or every 30 days if you don't. You will also be offered a **prepaid option**, in which the charge is deducted from your balance. If you run out of funds, Google will automatically stop the ads.

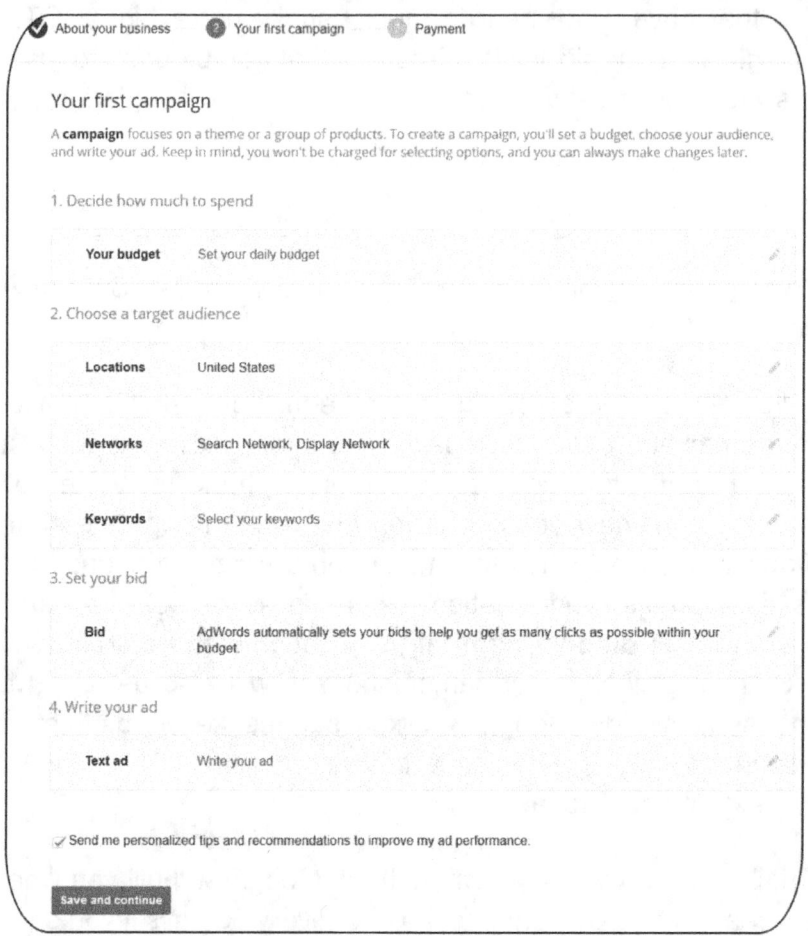

Google has free support that you can reach out to if there is anything you do not understand. If you contact Google from the "Help" section in your account, a customer service person will call you back free of charge, regardless of where you are.

Remember to **link your AdWords account** to Google Analytics. You do this by going to your AdWords account and then go to settings (symbol ⚙ in the upper right corner). On the drop-down menu, click on **Linked Accounts** and you will see a menu of accounts that can be linked to optimize your data. Now go to Google Analytics and click on "View details". Then go to, "Import site metrics" and save.

I recommend setting up a separate Search campaign and one Display campaign in the beginning. There are several types of campaigns available, but having one Search campaign and one Display campaign is the easiest way to start.

Give your campaigns names that are easy to understand. For example, if you are selling boats, it is better to call a campaign "Boats Search Campaign" instead of "Campaign # 1". This is both for your own understanding and, later down the line, to differentiate it from other campaigns when you contact Google support to get your campaigns to perform better.

You will have to choose the following parameters while setting up the campaign, but keep in mind that all details can be changed at any later time, so don't worry too much at this stage.

- Location – Where your ads will show geographically; this is set in U. S. and Canada by default. You can also exclude locations that are not interesting for your business. For example, if you are a local company in Philadelphia, why advertise in Mexico? This can be set up very precisely to an area of just a few miles.
- Languages – Corresponds to the language of your ads. AdWords looks at the language of the user's search query and Google language settings to place the ads.
- Budget – Can start as low as US $1.00 a day, based on your advertising goals and adjust it once you see your return on investment and what you are comfortable with.
- Bid strategy – What you are willing to pay for your ads. Google will have a default setting to automatically maximize conversions. I recommend leaving it at that for now.

- Ad extensions – Additional information you provide, such as location, phone number, further and supplementary descriptions or snippets, to increase reasons to choose your business, therefore clicking on your ad. This significantly increases your CTR and can be done at a later stage, if you choose to do so.

More information to come will look at Bid Strategy, Extensions and how they work.

Ad groups

It is to your advantage to organize your ads by a common theme, such as the types of products or services you want to advertise in ad groups. This will allow you to share sets of keywords, and the price or bid you are willing to pay for that keyword to trigger the ad. This is much more efficient than setting up keywords individually for each ad.

To create an Ad group, go to your campaign and click on "Ad group" then click on the "plus sign" (+) that appears, and Google will guide you on how to create your new Ad group. Go ahead, be creative and start making your first set of ads.

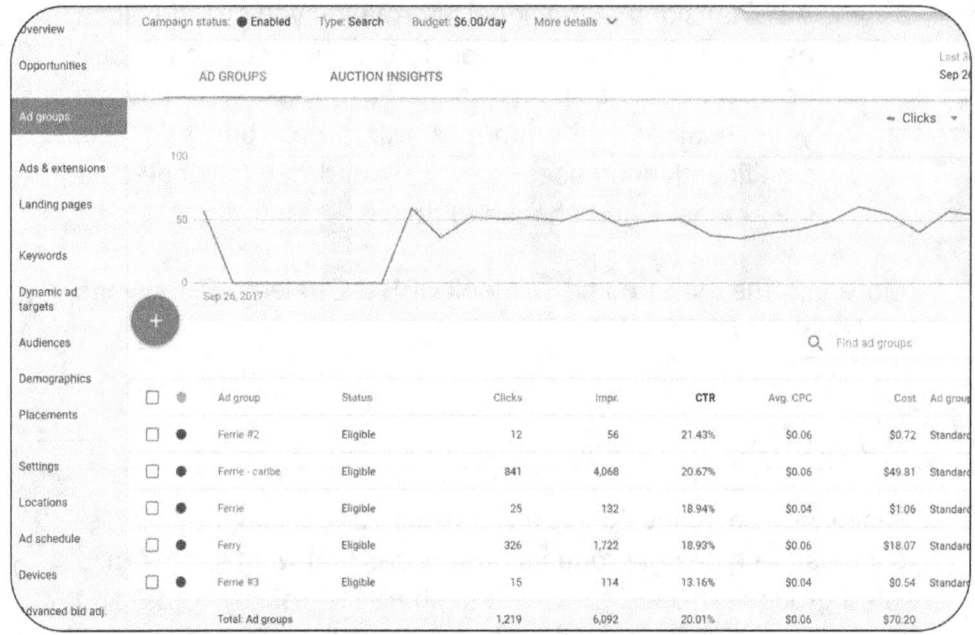

Keywords

Keywords are those words that are selected to trigger ads. There are different kinds of keywords, depending on how broad or exact you want the search to trigger the ad. Each has its own advantages and disadvantages. With a broader match, you attract a wider audience, but not necessarily the exact visitors you want.

There are four parameters called "Match Type" that can be set on keywords in the AdWords account. The Keyword Match Types are: Broad Match, Phrase Match, Exact Match and Broad Match Modifier.

- Broad Match. These keywords will give you the widest reach. This is the default setting in AdWords. Even if the user doesn't type the exact words or phrases, you will get a match on plurals, misspellings, synonyms, acronyms, etc.
- Phrase Match. This setting displays your ads only when someone's search includes the exact phrase of your keyword, or close variations with additional words before or after.
- Exact Match. Ads will appear on searches that match the exact word or close variations of that exact word. Using this, you might not receive as many impressions or clicks, but you'll probably see a higher click-through rate (CTR).
- Broad Match Modifier. With this choice, you can modify the keywords by adding a plus sign (+) in front of the Keyword and then the Ads will only show for exact words not synonyms. Any word with a + before it, must be in the search term.

Test all keyword match types in your campaigns to see which is getting the most clicks and best results. This will help you target users that are most likely to positively respond to your ads and thus avoid irrelevant traffic.

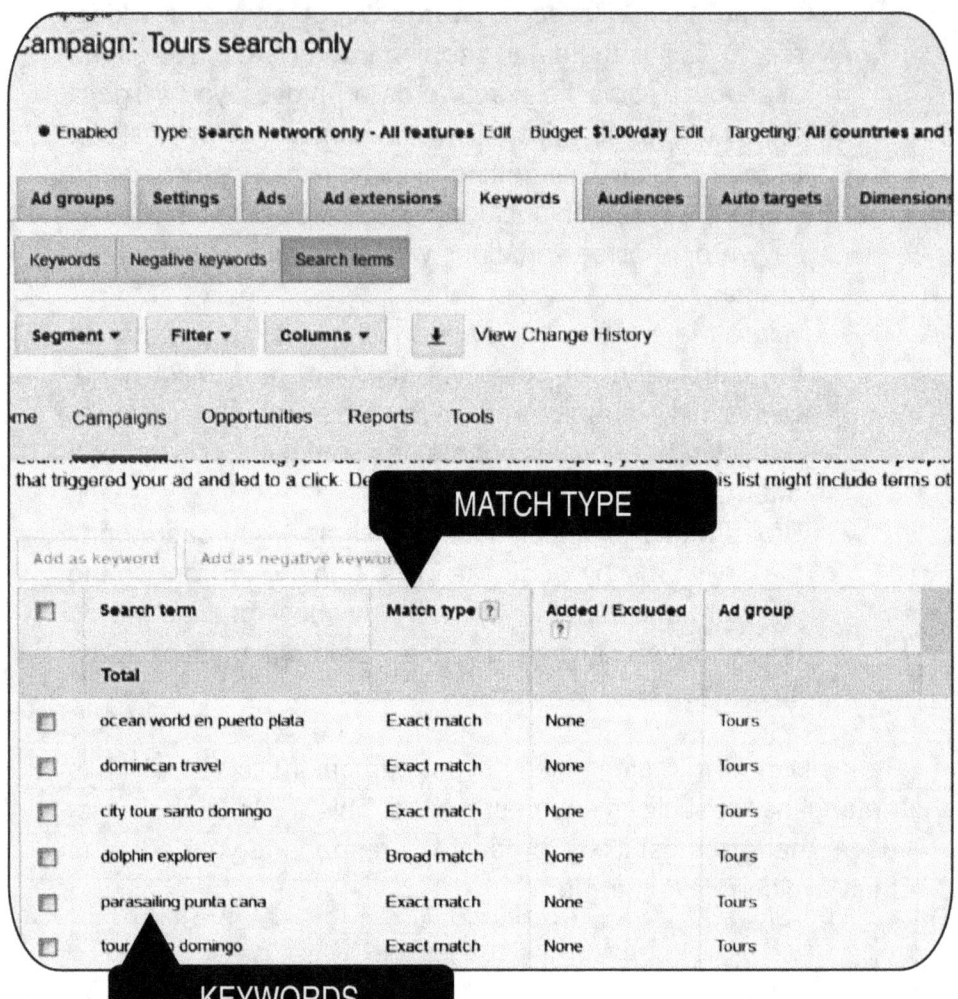

Importance of Negative Keywords

It is also important to use negative keywords to prevent ads appearing for the wrong search queries. The easiest way to know which negative keywords you should use is to check the actual search terms used to find your ad. You can then put your negative keywords on the list. These are the words that attracted to your ad user with no interest in your product or service. For instance, if you are selling Caribbean cruises, someone looking for employment on cruises might not be your target audience. By adding "employment on cruises," your ads will not show when people use that keyword combination.

How to add negative keywords - Log into your account and in your campaign, under the Keyword tab, go to "Search terms" and select with a check mark those you want to add as negative keywords to the list and save.

Other types of ads:

Dynamic Ads

Like the name suggests, Dynamic ads are those that change the headline of the ad according to your website content. This is not great if you have content that is constantly changing since content updates are not detected immediately. This can also generate a lot of unwanted traffic. A good way to keep tabs is to regularly monitor the search terms (that is, how people find your page) in all campaigns.

Call-only Ads

If your goal is to generate calls to your business, consider call-only ads. Ads created in call-only campaigns **show only on mobile devices** that can make calls. Clicks on these ads will only generate phone calls not clicks to webpages. You pay for the call, just as you pay for a click in a normal search campaign.

Home Service Ads

Emergency workers like plumbers, locksmith or similar can greatly benefit from the search ad network connecting advertisers to people actively looking for their products, especially in emergencies such as when a pipe breaks or someone is locked out.

Home Services Ads are specially designed for local house cleaners, locksmiths, plumbers, and other professionals that are prescreened to make sure that they are trustworthy. Introduced in 2015 and now available in Phoenix, Los Angeles, Riverside, Sacramento, San Diego, San Francisco, San Jose, Atlanta, Chicago, New York, Philadelphia, Dallas, Seattle and Washington, D.C., these ads are being rolled out in other cities at a fast pace. All advertisers using Home Service ads must complete a background check and the ads will display a Google's Green Shield Guarantee. The guarantee comes with an insurance policy of up to $2,000, if the job is booked through Home Services.

- With Home Service ads, you pay only for leads from customers that choose your business.
- You set a weekly budget that limits the total number of leads you receive in any given week.
- You may get a different number of leads from day to day, but you never spend more than your designated weekly budget.

Google has not announced a nationwide rollout of the program, but it is slowly adding more cities, so it is probably just a question of time before this will be available in a city close to you.

The program is accessible for the following services (though it might vary according to city):

Plumber
House Cleaner
Locksmith
Handyman
Contractor
Electrician
General Contractor
Painter

Garage Door Pro
Heating, Ventilation and Air Conditioning (HVAC)
Roadside assistance service
Auto glass service

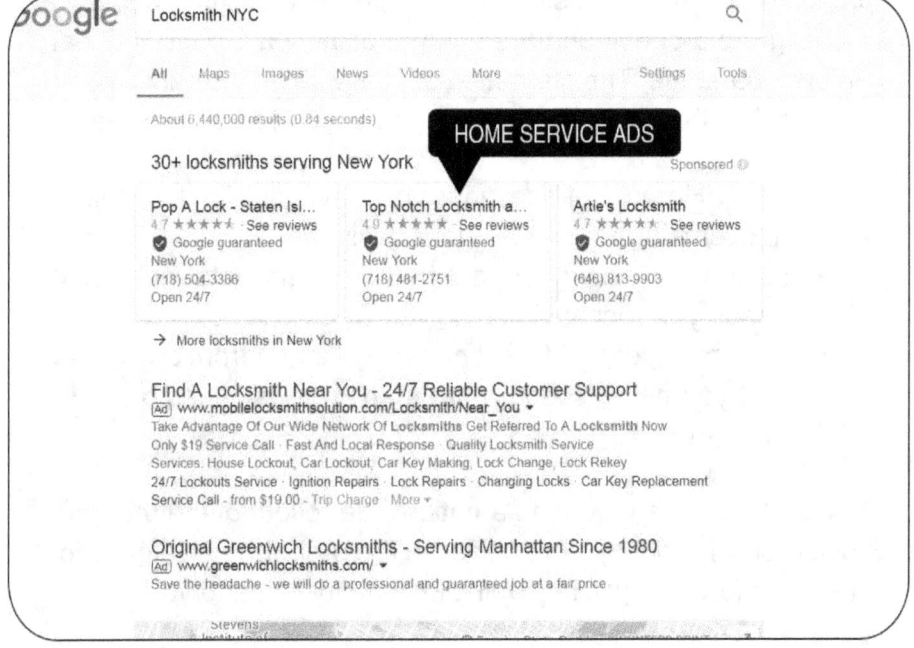

Testing Your Ads

If you want to test your keywords to see if your ads are showing, always do it by going into your AdWords account. Go to Tools - Ad Preview and Diagnosis. It is a mistake to try to test your ads searching in Google, since you will screw up your statistics and your CTR. Either way, you lose. If you do not click on your ad your CTR will go down and if you do, you will have to pay Google for the click.

Every single ad that is placed with Google is checked by a nit-picky person. He or she will check if the ad works and if the landing page has the same content as the ad. That person also checks if the ad follows Google's advertising policy on ethical guidelines. My experience, as a small advertiser, is that once Google thinks you are not complying with their ads policies, it is very difficult to make the company change its mind, even if you come up with new ads and change the content of the landing page. It is a waste of time to try change the review. Just scrap the ads and the campaign and start all over again.

Choosing a Bid Strategy

Your bid strategy is how much you pay for users to interact with your ads. To choose a strategy, you must have a clear goal for your page. Do you want to focus on getting clicks, impressions or conversions on your site?

There are many strategies but two basic ones:

Manual bidding, which requires you to set your own maximum cost-per-click bids. Use this type of bidding after you are very knowledgeable about your performance with Google AdWords.

Automated bid strategies Google will set bids for you based on your business goals. It's the simplest way to bid for clicks. All you have to do is set a daily budget, and the AdWords automatically manages your bids to bring you the most clicks possible within your budget. There are several automated bid strategies to choose from. You can set up experiments to see what works best for you. Google introduced at the end of September 2017 a new bid strategy called **Smart Bidding**. Basically, it is an automated bid strategy that is using Google's machine learning (Artificial Intelligence Technology) to deliver ads that are expected to perform better than other ads in your ad group.

Understanding the Google Ad Auction

The purpose of bidding on keywords is to win the auction, to get the ad to the top of the Google page when someone is searching. What you actually pay for is your position in the auction. The Ad Rank below you, divided by your quality score, equals the price you pay.

Quality Score

On a scale from 1 to 10, 1 indicates that the quality is very poor, so your ads will hardly show. This is calculated in every single auction. The most important part of a quality score is the CTR, because Google is relying on user feedback, where web users vote with their clicks. Relevance (to keywords and the search query) is the second component used to determine quality score. The third part is the landing page experience.

Google decides which ads to show and how they are positioned through the Ad Auction. The quality score combined with the maximum bid (for the ad) determines the Ad Rank which sorts the ads' position in the auction.

Google determines the Ad Rank by the bid, expected CTR, ad relevance, landing page experience, and the expected impact of extensions included in the ad.

In summary, to improve your ad position in the auction, you can:

- Improve the quality of your ads.
- Improve the quality of your landing page experience on computers and mobile devices.
- Increase your bid.

> *TIP:*
> *Better Ads = Better Ad Rank*
> *Quality Score X Max Bid = Ad Rank*

The amount paid for the bid is actually the amount offered by your competitor below you.

Since Google uses CTR as the most important metric to evaluate your Web page and rank it, it takes some time to generate enough traffic so that the quality of the page can be assessed. Any change to your page can easily take up to two weeks to have a real effect on the metrics of the site.

Analyzing The Metrics

As explained before, the science of analyzing web activity is called **metrics**. Google Analytics provides a series of reports that will tell almost everything about visitors to any site. Let's go through some of the most basic reports below.

The Audience Overview Report

This report provides an in-depth look at your traffic and the behavior of visitors once they arrive at your site.

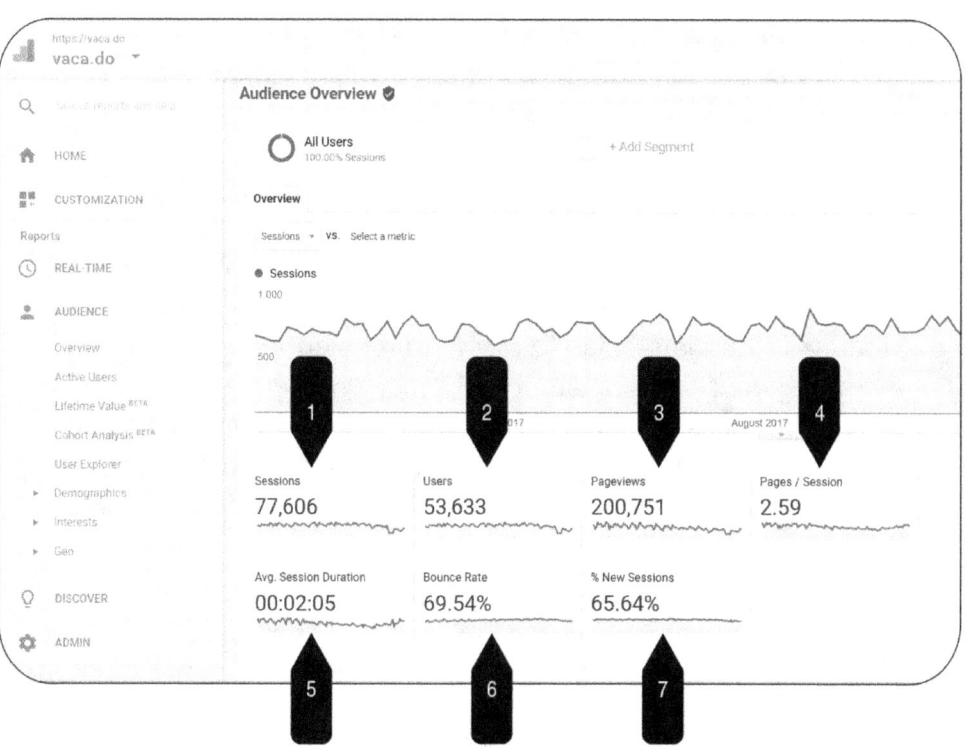

1. All events on your page are "Sessions."
2. Users are unique individuals that have initiated a session on your page.
3. Page views are the number of times pages on your website have been viewed.
4. Page/Session refers to how many pages are viewed on average during a session, also referred to as Page Depth.

5. Average session duration refers to the time spent on your page.
6. Bounce rate is the average single page session with no interaction on the page, which is usually 0 seconds. An acceptable bounce rate is less than 70%.
7. Percentage of new sessions refers to first-time visitors, people that have never been to your site before or more than two years without coming back.

Audience Report

Audience reports will help you understand more about the demographics of the visitors to your site. You can see age, gender and even their interests. This is the first step to see if you are attracting your specific target audience, which is very important for your overall advertising strategy. If you don't automatically see the report, you might have to activate it. Please go to: Admin - Properties - Enable Demographics and Interest Reports. It might take a day or so for the data to populate, once it has been activated.

If you have a local business, you want to make sure to contain your marketing efforts to the local area you serve. Remember you can target your ads to specific locations and see the geographical location of your users. This can be a great way to find untapped new markets in your territory.

Technology and Mobile are reports that let you know from what devices your visitors are accessing your site. For instance, if you see that your users are mostly coming from mobile devices, you might want to make a special mobile site.

The Acquisition Report conveys how your visitors are getting to your website. This information will help you make decisions on where to focus your marketing effort and tells you which channels provide the best conversion rate. Analytics tells you which campaign is generating the traffic to your website.

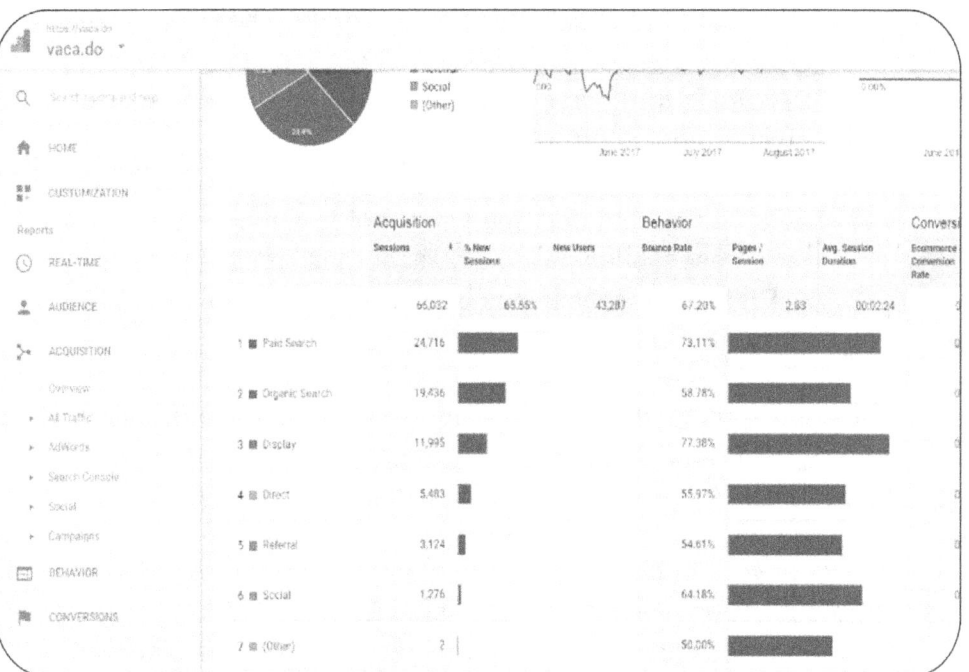

1. **Paid Search** refers to traffic coming from paid ads on the search network.
2. **Organic Search** means a visitor has found your page from a normal, unpaid search on Google or Bing--not by clicking an ad).
3. **Display** refers to a visitor that comes to your site by clicking an ad on the Display ad network. Usually, this is an image, video or rich media.

4. **Direct** refers to visitors that actually typed in your URL in their browser. These people have no doubt they want to go to your site. Sometimes, this direct traffic is reported as "None", because it does not come from another second-hand source, but directly.
5. **Referral** are links and visitors that come from other sites and not from a search engine. Those other sites might mention your site or provide a direct link to your page.
6. **Social** is traffic from Facebook, Instagram, Trip Advisor, Twitter and so on.
7. **Email** traffic is generated by an email campaign. That is an email that has been sent out to a long list of email addresses, often called a blast or mass mail. A link with a URL to your website has been in the email that has been clicked upon.

You can expand the links in the report to see more details about where the traffic came from. The best situation is to have a healthy mix of direct, organic and paid acquisitions.

You want your traffic to be of high quality. That means you want to have a low bounce rate, long session duration and many pages visited per session. Eventually, you want a high conversion rate. Usually, direct and organic traffic will have a lower bounce rate than the paid traffic. Compare the bounce rate from different channels to know what works and what does not.

Behavior report

This report will tell you what the visitors are doing on your website and what pages they are looking at. You can see the average time they spend on a page as well as the bounce rate for each one. This gives you a pretty good idea of the relevance of the page to the user. If there is a very low engagement on a specific page, you might want to improve the content.

You can also see the exact landing page where your visitor arrived on your site, and the last page this same person visited before exiting the site. It is good to monitor the **Behavior report** frequently to learn more about your site and where improvements are needed.

My all-time favorite report is **content in real-time**, where you can actually see what visitors are looking at in that instant. You can learn a lot from watching people's behavior on your site and see where the action is live.

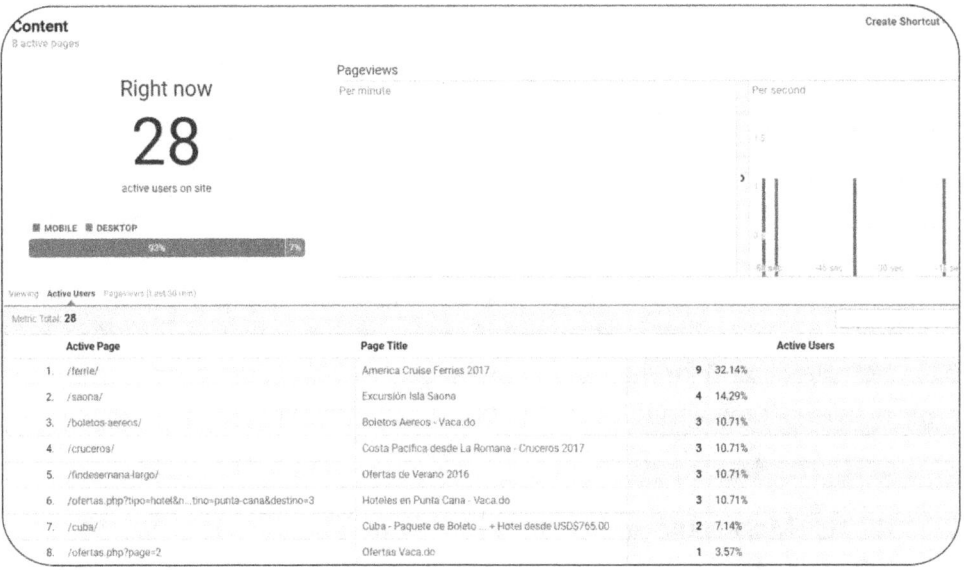

What do you do with your web visitor once she or he arrives at your site? There are myriad of options. However, you should always have what is known as a "Call to Action" option on the page. Visitors must have the possibility to fulfill their needs right there, whatever they might be: sign up for a subscription, buy something, receive a service, download an app, etc.

When a visitor makes a desired action on your webpage, it is called a **conversion.**

The conversion is always the ultimate goal of Internet marketing.

What is the cost per client?

When you pay for advertising on the Internet, you divide what you spend by the amount of conversions you get, and that is your cost per conversion. Better known as Cost Per Acquisition **CPA** (per client or event). This is the actual cost to get a client.

CPA = Cost Per Acquisition = money spent / clients acquired

Remember to frequently go to your page and try to improve it. It is very important that all the information be up-to-date. Also, you should visit competitors' pages and check how they do things. Having clear objectives of what you want to achieve with your website is vital for success. Your objective might be to generate a sale, a newsletter subscription, a tour booking, or you might simply wish to educate.

NOTE: Make sure to register your company with **Google My Business** so it will appear on Google maps and business listings. It is a free service that helps customers find you online.

What About Social Media?

Social media, such as Facebook, Instagram, YouTube, blogs and influencers, to name a few, can be an effective way to promote your business and there are many success stories with people and companies that have made it big with their creativity going viral. However, I strongly recommend you start concentrating on developing a solid website presence with relevant content, and use social media as a complement to your overall web presence and online brand.

This book will not go into social media advertising strategies but, rather, give you basic insights into overall Internet marketing. Social media has many ramifications and there is a world of ways to approach these platforms. Nevertheless, there are similarities between the advertising networks and the basic skills described in this guide. These, will help you understand the intricacies of social media advertising.

Advertising on social media means you are advertising on a Display Network, pure and simple, Such an ad shows images with some text in the form of ads or messages. It is also possible to do re-marketing on social media to visitors that have already been to your website. After searching the web, looking at a particular offer, it is very effective if you see an ad about that product or service on Facebook, Instagram and such.

Once again, pay a lot of attention to the landing page on your website, since the social media traffic must come to a place where it is easy to purchase your product or to engage with you and your services. My experience is that the selling and converting are best done on a website, at least when you start out.

Free Ads

Almost all the time Google has offers for new AdWords accounts, providing a credit. Take advantage of this and you can literally get your first month of advertising for free. To find the offer just Google: Google AdWords' coupon code advertising voucher

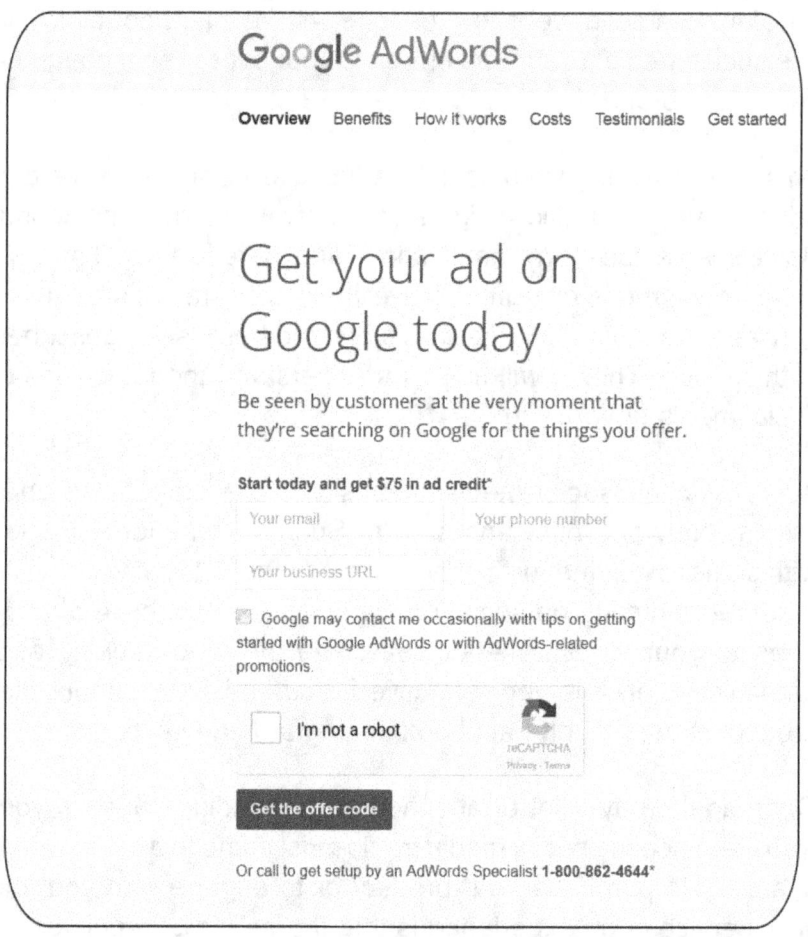

Tinkering With Your Campaigns

Once you see how your campaigns are performing, you need to optimize them. I want to keep this book basic, so I will only mention a few tricks to boost the performance.

After you have been running your ads for about 2 - 3 weeks, contact Google Support and ask how you can increase the ads' performance. If they have phone support available, the phone number appears in the help section. If the time is outside of support hours, fill out the support form. A specialist from Google will call you back and guide you through the best ways to optimize your campaigns. The AdWords Consultants can enhance your campaigns to your specific needs, You will learn a lot and your campaign will benefit a great deal from these chats.

Google allows the bids to be adjusted even down to specific devices. For instance, if you notice that a device is performing better than average (high CTR), you can increase the bid related to that particular device at a certain time of the day. It is a simple task. In your account, go to the settings tab, choose Devices and adjust the bid. This is a good way to improve campaign performance.

Automatic Notifications

Take advantage of Google AdWords' notifications that are automatically generated in the top right corner in your account. Check the notifications carefully. Even though they are generated automatically, they usually have very good advice and should be heeded.

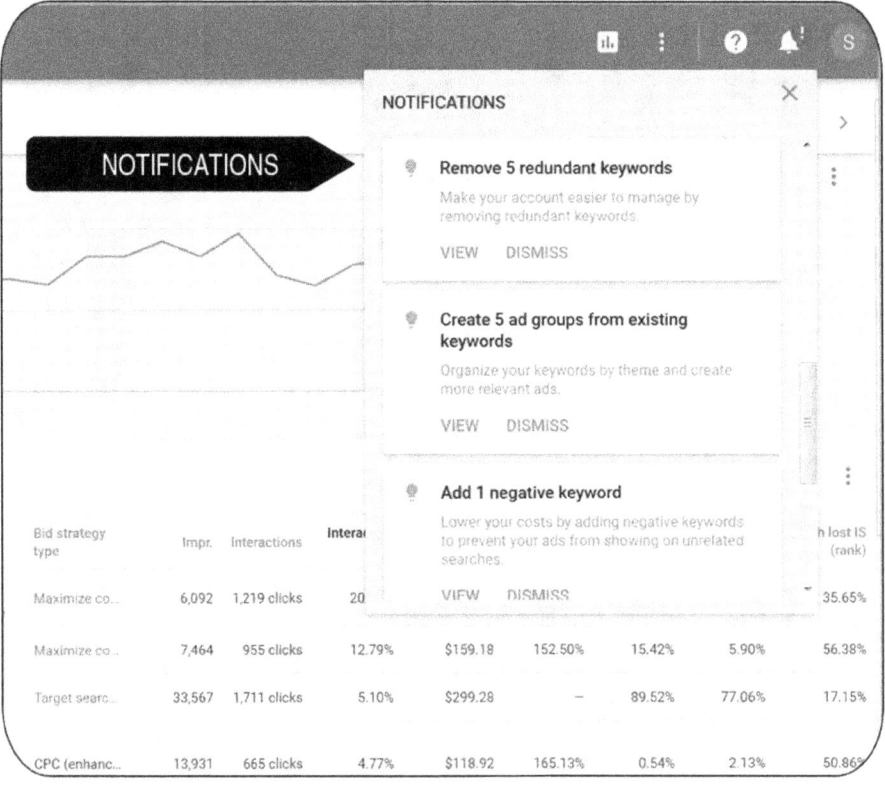

For display ads, which appear as images on the network, you can choose where you don't want your ad to appear. You might decide, for example, that you don't want to waste your hard-earned advertising budget on ads appearing below the fold, on error pages, or on parked domains.

How do you do it? While logged into your account, in a Display Campaign under **Display Network Tab**, go to the Placement Tab and scroll down to the bottom of the page. On the right, in **Site category options**, click the red button +OPTIONS. You will see a list of recommended exclusions. Just mark them and save.

Campaign placement exclusions			Site category options		
For account-wide placement exclusions, go to Shared library.			✦ OPTIONS Remove		
✚ EXCLUSIONS Remove Manage lists			☐	◉	Site category option
☐	◉	Placements ↑	☐	◉	Parked domains
☐	◉	admobapplicationnetwork.com	☐	◉	Error pages
☐	◉	adsenseformobileapps.com	☐	◉	Sensational and shocking
☐	◉	aldaba.com	☐	◉	Profanity and rough language
☐	◉	almomento.net	☐	◉	Tragedy and conflict
☐	◉	anonymous.google	☐	◉	Crime, police, and emergency
☐	◉	bajalealgo.net	☐	◉	Below-the-fold
☐	◉	lapulga.com.do	☐	◉	In-game
☐	◉	loteriasdominicanas.com			
☐	◉	Mobile App: Wordie (iTunes App Store), by ICO Group			
☐	◉	Mobile App: My Talking Tom (iTunes App Store), by Outfit7 Limited			
☐	◉	Mobile App: My Talking Angela (iTunes App Store), by Outfit7 Limited			
☐	◉	Mobile App: Wordie: Guess the Word (Google Play), by The FastMind			
☐	◉	Mobile App: My Talking Angela (Google Play), by Outfit7			

TIP:
Constantly create new ads to test against your best performing ads.

AdWords Express - A Simpler Way to Advertise

If you find AdWords to be complex and complicated, **AdWords Express** might be for you. Google launched AdWords Express in early 2017 as the "easiest way to advertise on Google". It has a very simple setup process, taking only a few minutes. To advertise on AdWords Express, you don't even need a website. You can direct all your ads to your Google+ page for more information on your business. AdWords Express will automatically manage your online ads and keywords without the need for any task or management. Keep in mind that this is not for complete campaigns, since it is only available for text ads on Google.com and Google Maps right now.

The ad auction runs automatically and your bid is assigned based on Google's bid auction model, so you do not have to worry about setting those. All you have to do is to place your budget. Google will also automatically target the ads based on your geographical location and specified category. Google's algorithm "will do the work so you don't have to". According to Google, you only need to dedicate 15 minutes a week to use AdWords Express.

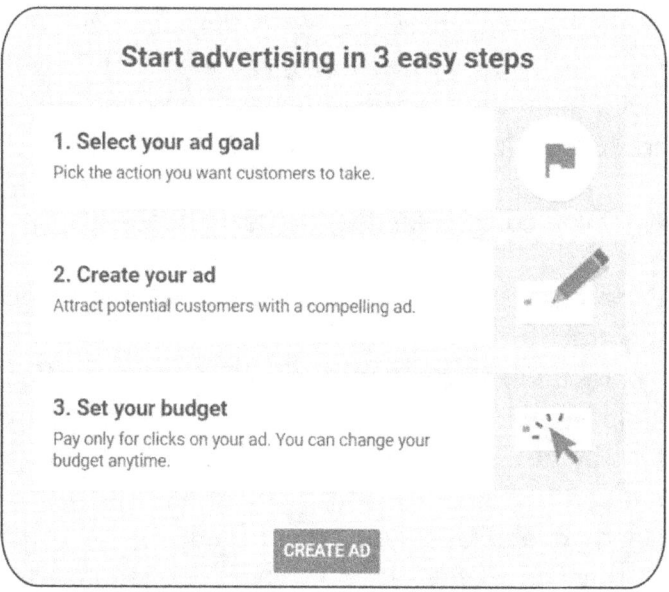

Google Beacon - Virtual World Connecting to Reality

Another project Google has been rolling out very low-key is Project Beacon by Google. It is a pilot program where Google sends beacons to businesses' physical locations to make the venues more visible to customers with mobile devices. Right now, the program is free for businesses.

Beacons are small one-way transmitters that send a unique one-way code from your venue to customers' phones to determine a user's location more accurately. This location information can be used in many ways on mobile phones. It can show how customers engage with the store. For example, you are most likely familiar already with "near me" searches, where you open your phone and conduct a search such as "coffee shops near me."

This is what you could potentially do using beacons:

- Broadcast the specials to all receptive smart devices in the area.
- Share, for example, how freshly brewed the coffee is.
- Help your business show up on personal maps with turn-by-turn directions people walking nearby on the street.
- Send updates about upcoming events.
- Collect photos, reviews, and other user-generated content for your business from people who've visited your store.

Right now, the project is only available in the US and UK, but more locations and features are expected to become available soon. In order to take part in the trial, you must receive a beacon from Google. If you're interested in receiving a beacon, request one here: https://services.google.com/fb/forms/projectbeacon bygoogle/

The Last Word

If you have come this far and implemented my recommendations, you are well on your way to benefit from a well-managed presence on the web. Congratulations!

A good way to learn more is to use the study guides that Google provides for free for their **exam studies** on the Google Partners Help page.

A Few More Advanced Tips

Use Dynamic Keyword Insertions

There are **two types of dynamic ads**. The first one was already described above; this is the type of ad assembled based on the content of your site. But you can also have the search query in the title of the headline of your ad. This is a very powerful tool as the ad will actually display what the visitor is searching for.

It is quite easy but requires a small knowledge to apply a code called snippet (copy and paste), so say you are selling bicycles and you want your ads to feature any query with interest in a Bike (triggering an ad that has Bike as a keyword). Just add this in Curly brackets- **{Keyword: bike}** in the headline of your normal text ad. This is an advanced feature so some caution is advised prior to using it. Be very careful using brand names. If you do not have permission there might be legal actions and the ads might not turn out as expected. So, we are back to my basic recommendations: monitor your search terms regularly to make sure your ads are responding to the search queries that you really want your ads to respond to. See page 37

Is Your Competition Out-Bidding You or Out-Smarting You?

To know if you are losing the bid auction due to low bids or by ad rank, check the Impression share (IS) of your campaign which is the percentage of times your ad appears, compared to the total times it could have shown. Add columns in your campaigns that will tell how you are doing.

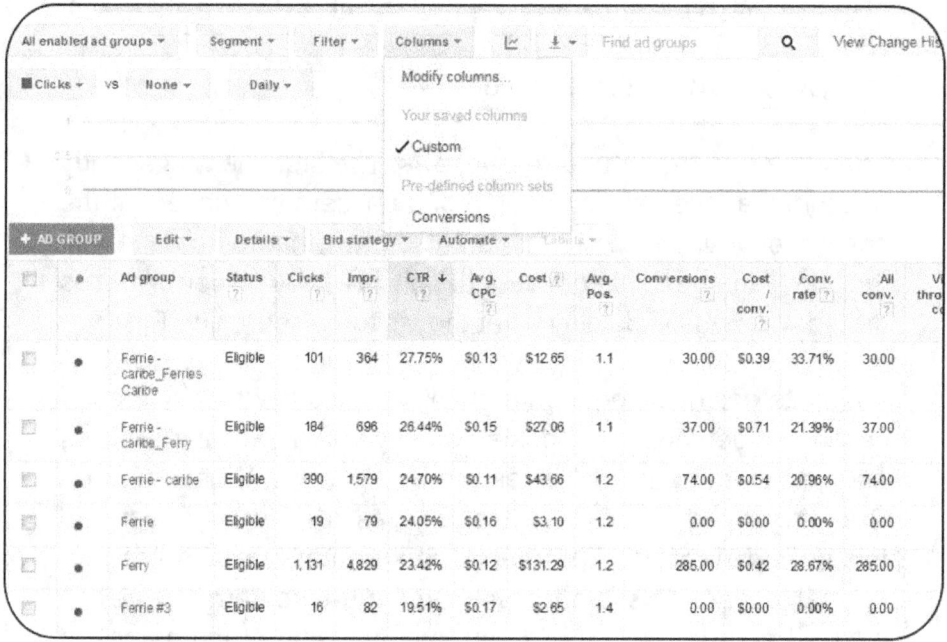

How to add columns to your campaigns: Go to the Columns tab and select Modify Column from the drop down menu. Click on Competitive Metrics - use the ↑ Search Lost IS (rank) and Search Lost IS (budget) to move the columns to the right. Click Apply to save the settings.

Last Comment

Take advantage of the Free Software Movement

The free software movement called Open Source is working to benefit computer users with the freedom to use, modify, build upon, and redistribute the software in any way you like. Free software puts its users in control.

There is an open source community where tens of thousands of talented people that work hard to create free software to be used and shared. The philosophy behind Open Source software movement is that software is not like other tangible products. Once a software is created, it can be copied many times with little cost. Free software means users are free to run, copy, distribute, study, change and improve the software.

You should take advantage of this and try to use Open Source in your daily life. There is Open Source software for almost anything you need. This book was written on an Open Source operating system (Linux / *Ubuntu*) and Google Docs.

I hope you enjoyed reading it.

Glossary

Above the Fold – What you see on your screen, without scrolling down.

Ad auction – The system used to select the position for each ad on a Google search page.

Ad group - A group of ads that share sets of keywords

AdWords Express - Simplified version of Google's search advertising

Algorithm – Instructions for a computer to follow in calculations and solving problems.

Analytics code – A small piece of JavaScript code that tracks the users' Web habits.

Backlinks – Links on other websites that recommend your page via a link pointing to your page.

Banner – Heading or advertisement appearing on a Web page.

Below the Fold – Part of a Web page not visible without scrolling down.

Bid – Offer at an auction.

Bid Strategy – An automated, goal-driven algorithm set to reach performance goals.

Black Hat SEO – Search Engine Optimization (SEO) techniques that try to trick the search engine to achieve a high rank for a page, thereby violating the search engines' terms of service.

Breadcrumbs – Graphical control element helping the user to navigate a website

Broad Match Modifier – An option that only shows ads in searches in which the word is designated with a plus sign (+).

Click-Through Rate – Impressions of an ad divided by the amount of Clicks it gets

CMS - Content Management System – An application used to create and modify digital content.

CPA or Cost Per Acquisition – The number of customers acquired for the money that was spent.

CPC or Cost Per Click – The amount of money spent divided by the clicks received.

CSS or Cascading Style Sheets – Used to set the visual style of web pages

CTR or Click-Through Rate is the amount impressions your ad gets divided by the number of clicks it receives

DNS or Domain Name System is translating human-readable names into IP addresses that consist of numbers to make them easier to remember.

Domain Name – Used to identify one or more IP addresses that are numerical addresses on the Internet.

Drupal – A popular Open Source Content Management System

Dynamic – Something that is constantly changing

Extensions – Extra information used to improve ads' performance.

Favicon – Short for favorite icon, displays a page's image next to the page's name in a list of bookmarks

GIF (Graphics Interchange Format) – Is a Bitmap image format

Google AdWords – Googles Pay Per Click online advertising platform

Google Analytics – World's leading platform for tracking and reporting website traffic.

Google Beacon - Bluetooth device that provides proximity-based experiences for users in the vicinity

Google My Business – Free service providing information about a business that appears on the right side of the search results

Google Page Rank – An algorithm used by Google Search to rank websites in their search engine results.

Google Panda – An algorithm aimed to lower the rank of low-quality sites.

Google Penguin – A ranking algorithm aimed to lower the rank of webpages not following Google's Webmaster Guidelines.

Google Tag Manager – A free tool that is used to manage, add and update website tags.

Google Web Designer – A free tool to create animated HTML5 images.

Home service ads – Special ads for services that have undergone a background check and can be awarded the Google guarantee.

Hosts – A network of servers that can be accessed over the Internet.

HTML or HyperText Markup Language – A coding language used to create Web pages.

IP Internet Protocol – Numerical label assigned to every device connected to the Internet.

JavaScript – A programming language.

Joomla – A popular Open Source Content Management System.

JPEG Joint Photographic Experts Group – Is an image format

JPG abbreviation for JPEG

KB kilobyte – 1,000 bytes.

Keywords – Words that trigger an ad or a search result.

Landing page – The page that is the entry point to a website where the visitor arrives.

Meta Data - information embedded on a page that helps a search engine understand the content and characteristics of that website.

Meta Description – Information used to describe the Web page's content.

Metrics – Measurement, collection, analysis and reporting of web data.

Negative keywords – Words that prevent ads from showing and advertisers from wasting money on ads that aren't relevant.

Open-source software – A license that provides the rights to study, change, and distribute the software to anyone and for any purpose.

Organic search results – Listings on search engine results pages due to relevance and not paid advertising.

Plugins – Software that is an add-on to a web browser to provide additional functionality.

PNG (Portable Network Graphics) – A graphics file format.

Pop-up – Automatically opens a new browser window to launch advertisements.

PPC or Pay Per Click – A form of paid advertising in which advertisers pay a fee for each click.

Quality Score – Is the total relevance of your keywords, ads, extensions and expected landing page experience.

Remarketing – Advertising directed to previous visitors to a Web page or their browsing history.

Search network – Search websites where ads can appear.

Search Query – The word entered to a search site as a request for information

SEO or Search Engine Optimization – Process of optimizing a website, so it can easily be found on the Internet.

Server – Large computer connected to the Internet to perform computing services.

Shared Libraries – Where AdWords stores the segmentation of visitors based on the way they have interacted with your site.

Snippet – Small blocks of code.

SSL or Certificates Secure Sockets Layer - Small data files that provide encrypted connection between the server and user to establish security as a digital signature.

Static - Lack of movement, or change.

SWF or Small Web Format – A small animation created with Adobe Flash.

Tags - In the digital marketing and analytics environment Tags are blocks of code that give information about the Web user.

URL or Uniform Resource Locator – An address on the Internet.

Web browser – Is a software application that is used for retrieving information on the World Wide Web

WordPress – A popular Open Source Content Management System.

XML or Extensible Markup Language – A file format for interchange of data over the Internet.

ZIP – A file format enabling archives to be compressed (made smaller) and then uncompressed (deflated) at a later time.

About the Author

 Sven Holmbom has entrepreneurship in his DNA and has been successful in the travel industry for over 25 years. Born and raised in Stockholm, Sweden, currently lives with his family in Santo Domingo, in the Caribbean island of Hispaniola. Avid sailor, mountain biker and lover of blue water fishing, he can now enjoy his passions all year round in paradise. He also holds a commercial pilot's license.

Sven has always been in the forefront of technological solutions and drawn to explore new ways of doing things. To be competitive in the travel business, he realized Internet marketing strategies became an essential part of doing business. He decided to share his knowledge through this book, after understanding that any business or service that wants to survive and grow in today's economy can benefit from applying the basic principles of Internet advertising and digital marketing.